Interesting Stories for Curious Kids

An Amazing Collection of Unbelievable, Funny, and True Stories from Around the World!

Cooper the Pooper

© **Copyright 2021 Cooper the Pooper - All rights reserved.**

The content contained within this book may not be reproduced, duplicated or transmitted without direct written permission from the author or the publisher.

Under no circumstances will any blame or legal responsibility be held against the publisher, or author, for any damages, reparation, or monetary loss due to the information contained within this book, either directly or indirectly.

Legal Notice:

This book is copyright protected. It is only for personal use. You cannot amend, distribute, sell, use, quote or paraphrase any part, or the content within this book, without the consent of the author or publisher.

Disclaimer Notice:

Please note the information contained within this document is for educational and entertainment purposes only. All effort has been executed to present accurate, up to date, reliable, complete information. No warranties of any kind are declared or implied. Readers acknowledge that the author is not engaged in the rendering of legal, financial, medical or professional advice. The content within this book has been derived from various sources. Please consult a licensed professional before attempting any techniques outlined in this book.

By reading this document, the reader agrees that under no circumstances is the author responsible for any losses, direct or indirect, that are incurred as a result of the use of the information contained within this document, including, but not limited to, errors, omissions, or inaccuracies.

Table of Contents

Introduction 1

The Shortest War in History 5

The Hole That Ate Helicopters 7

Dead Mice for Dental Hygiene 9

Lila: The Dog That Stopped a War 11

Russia Sells Alaska for Two Cents an Acre 13

The Bermuda Triangle: 'Nuff Said 15

Whose Mouse was Mickey? 19

Pineapples = Wealthy? 21

Wrestling Hall of Fame: Abraham Lincoln 23

The Boston Molasses Flood 25

Hans Island: Canada vs. Denmark 27

Operation: Acoustic Kitty 29

Golf on the Moon 31

The Galloping Crocs of the Sahara Desert 33

Ancient Rome's Many Uses of Urine 35

Potatoes Can Grow in Space 37

Australia's Great Emu War 39

The Emperor Scared of Rabbits 41

Death by Cherries 43

Naps Save Lives 47

The Leaning Tower of Pisa—Never Straight 49

Mansa Musa—The Richest Person in History 51

Lord Byron's Pet Bear 53

Animals of WWII—Juliana the Great Dane 55

Animals of WWII—Exploding Rats 57

Albert Einstein and Israeli Politics 59

The Stolen Brain of Albert Einstein 61

Sir Isaac Newton and the Apple 63

Man had Hiccups for 68 Years 65

The Mad Doctor—Dr. Semmelweis 67

Say "Cheese!" Now Hold for 8 Hours 71

Captain Jack Sparrow was a Girl 73

Final Words 75

Introduction

This book is a collection of short stories for children of all ages. You can read them yourself and tell your friends the stories the next time you see them. You can also ask Mom or Dad, or any adult or older sibling to read them to you. Either way, they are exciting and full of cool fun facts you can tell your friends about.

Let us go on a short and exciting trip through the history books to learn about the people, places, and events that have shaped the world we live in. Relive historical moments, meet people of the past; the geniuses, the not-so-sharp knives, the bullies, and the heroes who taught them kindness. Read about the adorable and brave animals that stopped and paused wars, and the really bizarre hygiene practices from ancient Egypt and Rome, and doctors who refused to wash their hands and stole brains.

Have you been to Italy to see the Leaning Tower of Pisa? Did you know that the Tower of Pisa is not just cool because it has stayed upright and somehow is not falling over? Italian scientist Galileo proved something important about gravity on the Tower of Pisa. Galileo dropped two balls that were different weights to prove that how quickly an object falls down does not depend on how heavy it is. An American astronaut on the space mission on Apollo 15 repeated a similar experiment on the Moon. He dropped a hammer and a feather, and they hit the ground at the same time. This was not the first time astronauts did something cool on the Moon. During Apollo 14, the commander astronaut played golf on the Moon!

Next time you put sugar in your tea or eat some sticky candy, try to imagine walking in the streets of Boston on a really hot summer's day. Can you smell the molasses?

Do you like cold or hot weather? Maybe you would like to live in Morocco with the desert and sea surrounding you. Or maybe you are more of a winter person and would rather live in Alaska and go skiing. If you brave through the cold, maybe you can reach Hans Island and see what the fuss is about and why Canada and Denmark do not want to give it up. If you took your own flag, maybe you could also claim the island as yours. Or maybe not because you will not find food there unless you have NASA's tubers and can grow potatoes. If they can grow in space, they can grow in the middle of two of the coldest oceans in the world.

Speaking of oceans, how many pirates do you think there are in the oceans? Did you know that pirates used to roam the seas and that there are stashes of treasure all over the world? If the oceans had an end, pirates would probably be the ones to find it! Maybe they know what happens in the Bermuda Triangle and how to come back. Have you heard about the mystery of the Bermuda Triangle? Do you have any conspiracy theories of your own about where all the ships and people go when they disappear? Maybe they go into another universe, and this is where all the dinosaurs and the galloping alligators also went.

Imagine how much the ground must have been shaking from Mansa Musa and his thousands of protectors from a thousand miles away. Can you imagine how happy the people were as he was handing them shiny pieces of gold while he was riding through the streets of Egypt? It must have been blinding!

If you were offered the presidency of a nation, what kind of president would you be? Would you be kind and honorable like George Washington, or smart and strategic like Abraham Lincoln? Or would you be worried and turn it down like Albert Einstein because you are not a politician? Can presidents only be politicians like Lord Byron? Can they also keep bizarre pets like bears? If you had to fight in the war, would you brave through and fight, or would you outsmart your enemies with spying equipment and maybe some super cats? I would run away like the Sultan of Zanzibar only two minutes after the fighting had started!

In this book you will find all these and so many more stories from all around the world (and space!) that are unbelievable, funny, a little scary, and all true. So buckle up and bring your friends (Mom or Dad can come too) along because we have a lot to learn!

The Shortest War in History

World War II, also known as the Second World War, lasted seven years, and between 40 million and 50 million people died during it. Seven years of constant fighting sounds like an extremely long time, but this was not even the 10th longest war in the history of the world. In every century, there were really long wars between different nations and groups of people, with the *Reconquista* being the longest war lasting 781 years!

European imperialism was a time when European nations set out to gain control over nations on other continents. Africa was the continent everyone wanted to control because it had lots of gold, diamonds, oil, cocoa and many other natural resources. For a while, Britain and Germany were fighting for many of the same places. They both wanted West Africa for the oil and cocoa, and they both wanted East Africa for the easy access to Asia where everyone was going to buy spices and silk. Then in 1890, Britain and Germany finally agreed to share East Africa and signed the *Heligoland-Zanzibar* treaty. This treaty gave Britain the island of Zanzibar off the coast of Tanzania, and Germany took control of the mainland country of Tanzania.

Britain immediately made Zanzibar a protectorate of the British Empire. A protectorate is a country that is under the protection and control of another country, but it still has its own leaders. In the case of Zanzibar, Britain made the Sultan a person they knew was a supporter of their ideas in 1893 to look after the area, and his name was Hamad bin Thuwaini. The Sultan is a powerful and respected leader, and the people do whatever the Sultan tells them. That is why it was important to the British that the Sultan would not give them any trouble and followed their orders. When Hamad died in 1896, and his cousin Khalid bin Barghash made himself Sultan without permission from the British, the British did not like this and began to prepare for battle when Khalid refused to step down.

Khalid and his forces of almost 3,000 men armed with artillery guns gathered around the palace. They also armed the Royal Yacht, which was in the harbor nearby. Similarly, the British sent their soldiers to make sure the people would not fight in the streets of Zanzibar. On the evening of August 25, 1896, the chief British diplomat Basil Cave sent a message to Khalid in the palace telling him to bring down his flag and give himself up by 9:00 the next morning. If he didn't, the British troops would open fire on the palace. Khalid refused, and at exactly 9:00am on August 26, 1896, the order was given. By 9:02am, most of Khalid's artillery had been destroyed, and it is said that this is also the time he escaped through a back entrance and ran away. His forces and the servants continued the fight until they were defeated at 9:40am. The shortest war in history had begun and ended in just 38 minutes.

Khalid escaped that time, and he was helped by the Germans to run away to mainland Tanzania where they protected him even though the *Heligoland-Zanzibar* treaty meant that the British rulers had the right to go fetch him and arrest him. Eventually, Britain invaded Tanzania, and Khalid was finally captured and sent to exile in the island of Saint Helena. After some time, Khalid was allowed to go back to East Africa, and he died in Tanzania in 1927.

The Hole That Ate Helicopters

Humans have defied the laws of nature and built many impressive things. There are world records for the tallest building, the largest dam, and many other buildings. Some are so big, like the Great Wall of China, that you can see them from space. At 1,722 feet (525 meters) deep and 3,900 feet (1.25 kilometers), the Mirny Mine is one of the largest manmade excavations in the world, and it is both so large and deep that it can suck in helicopters. How does it do this, you ask? Gravity!

The Mirny Mine is a gigantic open-pit Kimberlite diamond mine in Eastern Siberia. This area used to be part of the Yakut Autonomous Soviet Socialist Republic which was in the United Socialist Soviet Republic (USSR). After World War II, the USSR was economically ruined, and when geologists found deposits of Kimberlite that led to the digging of Mirny Mine, the region got a needed economic boost.

Kimberlite is a rock that is the most common carrier of diamonds, and it is named after the South African town of Kimberley, which is where a diamond weighing 83.5 carat (16.70 g) was found in 1869. This diamond was named the *Star of South Africa,* and its discovery was what led to the big diamond rush and the digging of the first open-pit mine in South Africa called the Big Hole. Open-pit is a method of mining where geologists will dig a hole—the pit—once they have discovered a mineral at a place. This method of mining is much cheaper than other kinds of mining such as shaft mining. This is because it takes less workers and machines to operate an open-pit mine. On top of that, you can extract the ore much quicker, and more of it can be taken out of the ground at a time than in a mine that needs more energy and machinery.

Open-pit mining is used when the minerals are close to the surface and there is no need to dig tunnels. So why is Mirny Mine an open-pit mine but runs so deep? In geological terms, "close to the surface" does not mean distance you can dig with a normal garden shovel. In fact, Kimberlite is found between 93 and 280 miles (150 and 450 kilometers) under the ground. That is still quite deep, and that is why diamond mines, even when open-pit, are still large and deep. This explains the gravity part. There have never been confirmed reports of the Mirny Mine sucking in a helicopter because the airspace above the mine is closed to all aircraft, but it is very likely.

If you dig a large enough hole into the earth, the air inside the hole starts to get warm as you get close to the very hot center of the earth. The deeper the hole, the warmer the air will be. This is fine, except the air directly above the hole is now cooler than the air inside the hole, and according to physics, warm air rises and cool air sinks. So there is a lot of movement as the Earth tries to balance this difference in temperature. This happens very quickly. Now imagine a helicopter trying to fly over this whole. First, the warm air will lift the helicopter, but the cool air above it will want to sink the helicopter. The pilot will not have enough time to increase the spin rate of the rotors to work against the sinking motion by the air. Before you know it, the helicopter will likely spin out of control downwards, and it might hit the side of the hole and fall in. Though this hasn't happened yet due to safety precautions, it is still possible!

Dead Mice for Dental Hygiene

Did you know that doctors place maggots on burn wounds to clean the area because maggots eat all the burnt and dead skin and leave the healthy skin to heal and grow back? That sounds very gross, but it works, and there is still no modern replacement that does the job better. There is another pretty gross medical practice that was popular in ancient Egypt, and thank goodness we don't do it today: dead mice.

There were two ways to go about using dead mice to treat dental issues. For toothaches, ancient Egyptians used to mash up dead mice into a paste which was then applied to the decaying tooth to relieve the pain and also cure the decay. If the toothache was severe or if the problem was only the gums, they would slice open a mouse, and while it was still warm, keep it on the affected area.

Dental hygiene in ancient Egypt was important because the people were suffering from poor dental health such as tooth decay and gum disease. It was mainly because of the food they ate and because many people were not taking care of their teeth. Ancient Egyptians generally ate a lot of raw vegetables and hard breads that wore the enamel on their teeth down. Also, there was sand and tiny stones in their bread because of their location. Many desert nations used to struggle with these issues because the sand is everywhere and very hard to keep out of food, especially grains like wheat. And where does their bread come from? All that sandy, rocky wheat. Gross!

Ancient Egyptians knew how important oral hygiene was to the overall health of a person, and they invented the earliest kind of cleaning powder for teeth made of crushed rock, salt, mint, pepper, and dried iris flower. In a sense, this was some of the first ancient Egyptian toothpaste! However, this caused their gums to bleed because of the rocks and harsh ingredients like salt and pepper, but they were on the right track. Many of the active ingredients in toothpaste today come from this long line of trying things until they work. Over time, the Egyptians moved from stones to salt and crushed eggshells as abrasives because they were less harsh, and today we use much gentler abrasives like calcium carbonate. We also use fluoride to protect the enamel on our teeth and to fight cavities.

Archaeologists have found metal bands around the teeth of some of the mummies studied, and this shows that the idea of dental braces was already popular in ancient Egypt to create pressure around teeth to prevent tooth loss. Even more interesting is their findings of teeth that look like they were reattached using gold or silver wire.

Visits to the dentist now are one of the most important health care responsibilities we have, and even though very few people enjoy going to the dentist, it is much more comfortable than it was in the time of ancient Egypt.

Lila: The Dog That Stopped a War

The year is 1777, and Founding Father and then general of the colonial army of America, George Washington, has just experienced one of the most important and humbling battles during the American Revolution. He also realizes that there is a new member in his group: a dog. In fact, this was the British General's fox terrier Lila, and she was the reason for pausing the battle.

The Battle of Germantown is one of the few battles Washington and his men lost, but it also gave them the motivation to continue fighting for the freedom of the American colony from British control. During the battle, the commander of the British Army, General Sir William Howe, kept dogs with him, and many other generals including George Washington also took their dogs to battles.

One day, the Continental Army tried to catch the British Army by surprise, but there was too much confusion, and Washington's men started shooting at each other. The British realized what was happening and defended their camp successfully, forcing the Continental Army to retreat. In the confusion following the Continental Army's failure to attack the British camp, Lila ended up at Washington's camp, and they knew the dog belonged to Howe because she had Howe's name on her collar.

Washington's men saw this as an opportunity to get back at the British for losing the battle, and they told Washington to not return Lila, instead suggesting he use her to gain leverage against Howe. Washington did not like these ideas and took care of Lila until he could return her. As if that was not nice enough, he asked his right-hand man and fellow founding father Alexander Hamilton to write a polite note to Howe. Washington then declared a ceasefire, which is when soldiers in battle pause the fighting, to have one of his helpers take the dog and the note under a flag of truce to the British camp. The note read, "General Washington's compliments to General Howe, does himself the pleasure to return him a Dog, which accidentally fell into his hands, and by the inscription on the Collar appears to belong to General Howe."

This was clearly an act of kindness, no matter what Washington's reasons were for doing it. Some historians argue that he was just being a nice and kind gentleman and that he was not using this unique situation to his advantage. This is not hard to believe because Washington really loved dogs, and there are many historians who have written about his own dogs and how he used to treat the dogs of other generals in his encampment. However, another group of historians believe while it was nice of him to return Lila to Howe, he was doing so to spy on the British and study their camp through the helper he had sent with the dog.

Whatever the reason was, Lila became well-known as the dog George Washington called a ceasefire to return safely to her owner. The colonial government praised Washington for this act of kindness and gave him a medal. We don't know for sure what happened to Lila after that, but it is very likely that she went back to England with Howe when the general resigned after the Battle of Germantown.

Russia Sells Alaska for Two Cents an Acre

On a clear day and from a high enough point, you can see Russia from Alaska. The cool part is, Alaska used to belong to Russia. On the map, however, Alaska looks like it would be a part of Canada because it borders the Canadian province of British Columbia, and one of Canada's three territories, Yukon. Instead, the state of Alaska is one of the 50 United States of America (USA).

From about 1733 until 1867, Russia controlled most of what we know as Alaska today. Back then, it was called Russian America. The Russian government sold the land when they realized that they could not defend themselves from an invasion from Britain if they attacked Alaska. At the time, Russia had an old fight with Britain, and when the United States bought Alaska, they also inherited this fight with Britain. The reason Russia sold Alaska to the United States and not Canada, even though geographically it would have made more sense, is because Canada was controlled by Britain at the time. This also explains Russia's fear of invasion from Britain because it could either come through the Bering Sea or the Canadian borders.

In 1867, Secretary of State William Seward and Russia's Minister to the United States Edouard de Stoeckl signed the *Alaska Treaty of Cessation*. This treaty meant that Russia gave up its ownership and control over Alaska and sold it to the United States. From 1867 to about 1884, this area was known officially as the Department of Alaska. It is important to know that through all of this, as Alaska changed hands between Europe and the Americas, its native people called the Aleut were always there, and they always called their land *Alaxsxaq* or *Alyeska* which means 'mainland' because it is bordered by the Arctic Ocean in the north, the Pacific Ocean in the south, and the Bering Strait and Sea in the west.

Throughout the late 1880s, Alaska went from being named the District of Alaska to the Territory of Alaska for the better half of the 1900s because its importance and place in American history changed. Then in 1959, the United States declared Alaska a state, making it the 49th state, and it became the largest state of the United States in area. In fact, it is so large in area that the state of Pennsylvania could fit into it 14 times.

The United States got very rich when gold was discovered in Alaska in the 1890s. It is hard to say if Seward knew about the gold before he bought the land of Alaska for the United States. We also cannot say if Alaska was made an official state because the United States government knew of the presence and ultimate discovery of oil in 1968 at Prudhoe Bay. This discovery eventually led to the installing of the Trans-Alaska Pipeline completed in 1977 that led to the oil boom in the area. Either way, buying Alaska was a politically and economically good decision by Seward that still benefits the United States to this day.

The Bermuda Triangle: 'Nuff Said

The very idea of ships and aircraft just disappearing into thin air is bizarre, but there are degrees to the madness and some stories about the Bermuda Triangle are less believable than others. The most famous story, and maybe the reason the mystery around the Bermuda Triangle has been kept alive, was the disappearance of *Flight 19*. There were a total of 5 aircrafts with 14 men in the United States Navy training off the coast of Florida on December 5, 1945. When the control room could no longer talk to the crew leader of *Flight 19*, the Navy even sent a Martin Mariner airplane to search for the missing aircraft, but that plane and 13 men who were part of its crew also disappeared.

The Bermuda Triangle is said to be anywhere between 500,000 square miles to 1.5 million square miles of sea in the Atlantic Ocean. It starts off the south-eastern coast of the United States of America where Florida is, goes all the way to the Island of Bermuda on one corner, and ends in Puerto Rico on the other corner, making a triangle shape. Aircraft and boats of different sizes have disappeared all throughout the Bermuda Triangle, which is why it is so difficult to explain what causes these disappearances because there is no specific section of the Triangle where things start to disappear. This also means scientists cannot test where the disappearing zone starts because it can be pretty much anywhere at any given time.

The Bermuda Triangle is a busy shipping route that connects North America, the Caribbean, and Europe with vessels crossing every day. Yet more than 1,200 ships and more than 320 aircraft have disappeared within its 'borders' since 1930. There is no real explanation for why some ships and planes disappear and others do not, and it does not help that in many of these disappearances, no wreckage was found. It really looks like these ships and planes just vanished, and because the seas are so understudied, we simply do not know what is happening.

There have been many hypotheses using the laws of physics, historical records, and ongoing research from divers from all over the world trying to understand what happens in the Bermuda Triangle. For starters, many of the pilots flying the planes that have gone missing did not give out distress signals to the control officers communicating with them. This means they did not see anything unusual or unsafe enough for them to let the control officers know they were in trouble. Most importantly, the pilots were highly trained and skilled and would not have made small mistakes that would have led to accidents. Plus, rescue teams never found any wreckage or missing people.

The case of *Flight 19* is more interesting because the flight instructor Lieutenant Charles Carroll Taylor did communicate that he was lost, and it was believed that he flew the crew out to sea by mistake until they ran out of fuel and crashed. This was odd because he had done the exact same flight under similar conditions many times before and had a very good knowledge of the ocean around Florida. One of the largest sea searches in history started, and the wreckage of *Flight 19* was never found. Years later, Lieutenant Charles was proven innocent of wrongdoing, and the tragedy of *Flight 19* was concluded as a result of an 'unknown' cause.

Some people believe there are spirits, ghosts, or giant sea creatures causing these disappearances. What do you think? Could it be a perfectly normal explanation of physics we have yet to find the equation to solve? Or maybe there is a gigantic empty hole in the sea we have not yet identified, and maybe you can be the scientist to find it and finally solve the mystery of the Bermuda Triangle? Until then, the world may never know!

Whose Mouse was Mickey?

When we hear the name Walt Disney or even just see the Disney logo, the first thing that comes to mind for most of us is Mickey Mouse. Not only is Walt Disney's name and legacy on Mickey Mouse, but he also played the voice of Mickey Mouse in the famous animations. When asked how he came up with such a brilliant idea, Disney has told a few stories that are different from each other, and some are not very convincing. So it made sense when it was revealed that Walt Disney did not, in fact, create Mickey Mouse. Not alone, anyway. Certainly not the drawing and animation.

The person truly behind the iconic Mickey Mouse drawing is animator Ub Iwerks who grew up in Kansas City where he and Walt Disney met when they were teenagers. They became good friends and started working on many projects together. The two men owned and worked at the Laugh-O-Gram Studio and brought young creators and animators together to design and make animations. This is the same studio Walt Disney has said was the origin story of Mickey Mouse. He said it all started with a pet mouse he had there. Walt Disney was very charismatic, and people liked hearing him speak. He also enjoyed being listened to and spent a lot of time making himself and his stories entertaining even in his real life when he was not playing the character of Mickey.

In 1928, Walt Disney lost the rights to his first famous character, Oswald the Lucky Rabbit. His animators did not want to continue working with him because they thought he was going to fail. Ub Iwerks had created Oswald the Rabbit with Disney, so Iwerks was the only animator who stayed with Walt Disney. As the other animators were finishing Oswald for the last cartoon, Iwerks and Disney were working in secret creating a new character. Iwerks designed Mickey Mouse all by himself after sketching 700 drawings a day. From this design, Iwerks then animated the first Mickey Mouse cartoon only in two weeks, something that would have taken most other animators months to complete.

Iwerks was able to do that because he was incredibly talented, but he also had the advantage of being both the engineer and designer, so he could do everything all by himself, and he did.

The reason Disney became famous as the genius behind Mickey Mouse while the true creator Iwerks remained in the shadows is that Walt Disney told so many dramatic stories where he told everyone that he was the one who designed Mickey Mouse. As the character and animation grew, he could not tell the truth. Who knows? Maybe he did not even want to. We can take comfort in knowing that in the end, the rightful creator of Mickey Mouse received the credit he deserves even though it came over 70 years later. Moreover, we can enjoy Ub Iwerks' talent in Disney's special effects and some of his greatest works such as *101 Dalmatians*, *Sleeping Beauty*, *Mary Poppins*, and *The Birds*.

Pineapples = Wealthy?

If pineapples were as valued today as they were in the 18th century, one would cost about $8,000.

We often hear of how cheap gold was one hundred years ago compared to now, and how Grandpa could buy a full tasty lunch and snacks for only $1. We can explain this quite easily: When something like gold is discovered or new money is created, it is because there is a big need for it. Take gold for example. When new gold deposits are discovered, a lot of people want it, and most of the people who live near where it was found will be able to have it because there is a lot of it. Then, a few people from further away will hear about this discovery and start traveling to the place of discovery to also get some gold for themselves. Depending on the size of the area of deposits, it can be up to many years of increased digging before they start to run out of the gold, or it starts being deeper and deeper in the ground. This is how many mines all over the world were built. Instead of individual people, companies also hear about the gold found in the area, and they go there to set up a large mine.

When the gold on the surface is all gone, the only way to find gold is by using heavy and expensive machines, and all the people who want gold will now have to buy it from the mine, and the mine owners will begin to increase prices. Soon, gold will become really expensive and hard to buy, and somehow this makes it even more wanted. The gold has gained value.

So how do things *lose* value, then?

Well, the opposite happens. Someone figures out how to make something that used to be found in small amounts easy to find or make. Sometimes this might even be caused by nature. When the weather changes after many years, some plants might start growing where they used to never grow, or some that used to grow only in the summer might start growing the whole year. This is proof of a long process called climate change, and that and science give us the knowledge to grow tropical fruits like bananas and pineapples in places they were not originally found in.

When Christopher Columbus arrived on the Caribbean island of Guadeloupe in 1493, he was fascinated by a mysterious spiky and sweet fruit that had made its way there from South America. Columbus took some pineapples with him back to Spain, and the people there liked the sweet fruit. They tried to grow them, but pineapples are a tropical fruit, which means they can only grow naturally in a place that is warm throughout the year, and Europe is not. So the only way the Spanish could get pineapples was by going to the Caribbean islands, a long and dangerous journey across the Atlantic Ocean.

Spanish royalty and artists really liked pineapples, and they reached England in the 1700s. Because they had already heard how difficult it was to get this mysterious fruit, the English immediately saw pineapples as a sign of wealth, and the less wealthy people liked them so much that sometimes they would even rent a pineapple if they could not afford it and show it off at their parties.

Wrestling Hall of Fame: Abraham Lincoln

Do you ever wonder what presidents used to do before they became presidents? Abraham Lincoln was a wrestler when he was young before he was elected as President, and he was inducted into the National Wrestling Hall of Fame in 1992. This on its own is not the impressive or surprising part because other presidents have also been in this Hall of Fame. These include Founding Father and the first president of the United States George Washington, Founding Father John Adams, and Theodore 'Teddy' Roosevelt.

Abraham Lincoln was the 16th president of the United States of America and served as president from March 4, 1861 until he was murdered on April 15, 1865. In these four years, he became known as honorable and determined. His presidency began and ended during the Civil War, and there were constant threats on his life, and his presidency ended with his murder. Abe Lincoln, as he is affectionately known, began the difficult and important road to freeing slaves with the signing of the Thirteenth Amendment even though it was only passed after his death. Lincoln also used his professional training as a lawyer to build the foundation of laws that took care of the poor people in the United States, allowing them to live in the parts of the country where they could work and support themselves.

As a young man and wrestler, he was a slightly different person. He was six feet and four inches (1.93metres) tall, 185 pounds (83.9 kilograms), and very strong. He was very good at hand-to-hand combat and finding the weaknesses of the people he was fighting against. Some historians think this skill helped him later in his role as president. In fact, Abraham Lincoln gained supporters in his early campaigns for a United States Senate seat in Illinois in 1858 because people had heard about his talent as a wrestler. Although he lost the election in that round, two years later he won the presidency partially because the public had grown to like him because he was a competitive wrestler but also a fair and honest sportsman. These are some of the most important life qualities, and they tell us a lot about a person.

Another reason Lincoln was so highly respected and more impressive than the wrestlers of his time—and even more than the other former presidents who were skilled wrestlers—is the fact that he was a wrestler for 12 years and fought about 300 matches. As if that is not enough, he has only ever lost 1 of the 300 matches! Despite this single loss in 1831 to a man named Hank Thompson, the legend of the wrestler who could out wrestle, outrun, and throw down anyone in Illinois lived on.

Abraham Lincoln, along with eight other former presidents of the United States, can be seen in an exhibition titled "Presidential Grapplers" at the National Wrestling Hall of Fame and Museum. However Abraham Lincoln alone enjoys the special honor of "Outstanding American". How many people can say they have been a successful lawyer, almost-undefeated wrestler, and possibly the best president of their country's history?

The Boston Molasses Flood

When you think of floods, I bet you never imagine it could be molasses flowing down streets! Sadly, that is exactly what happened on January 15, 1919, in Boston, Massachusetts. A storage tank full of 2.3 million gallons (87 million liters) of molasses burst, and the molasses flooded the streets at speeds of 35 miles per hour (56 kilometers per hour). This tragic accident left 150 people injured and killed 21 people.

To understand how this happened, we need to first find out what molasses is and how it behaves in different environments.

Molasses comes from sugarcane plants, and it is used to make sweet syrup amongst many types of sweeteners. Molasses can be found in many countries with large sugar plantations like Brazil, India, and Thailand. When molasses is fermented, it can make alcohol. Fermentation is a process where a fruit, vegetable, or a mixture is left in a dark warm place to make good bacteria grow. Alcohol is the result when sugar is fermented, and when you introduce a difference in temperature, the mixture can start a chemical reaction that can cause an explosion. This is what happened and caused the big disaster in the neighborhood of North End in Boston.

The temperatures in Boston in the week leading up to the explosion were very cold because it was right in the middle of the winter. Then suddenly on January 15th, temperatures rose above 40 °F (4 °C). This is still quite low, but a ship had delivered fresh molasses on January 14th. Every time a fresh load of molasses was delivered in the winter months, it had to be heated to make it flow easily because the cold tank would make it a little hard and difficult to take out. When the tank warmed up suddenly, the older, colder molasses expanded, and when the new warm molasses was poured into the tank, this caused an expansion, and that is what led to the tank bursting open. The weight of the molasses collapsed the tank and this, and the fact that it was warmer, is what allowed it to flow out at such high speeds.

The tank belonged to the United States Industrial Alcohol Corporation, and after the accident, 119 people sued the company for damages and losses of life. The company's lawyers claimed that the explosion was caused by Italian anarchists bombing the tank. The judge ruled that the United States Industrial Alcohol Corporation was to blame for the accident because they had known for three years that there were leaks in their tanks, and they painted them brown to hide the fact that the tanks were unsafe. The company was ordered to pay about $630,000 in damages with the relatives of the people who died receiving about $7,000.

It took weeks and many people to clean up the sticky streets using salt water from a fire boat and then throwing heaps of sand to absorb the molasses. Everything was sticky, and to this day, people living in Boston say they can smell the molasses in the street during very hot summer days.

Hans Island: Canada vs. Denmark

Hans Island is a large piece of rock that lies exactly in the middle of the Nares Strait, a channel of sea connecting the Atlantic Ocean and the Arctic Ocean. The Nares Strait is 22 miles (35.4 kilometers) long, and it separates two countries: Canada and Greenland which is a territory of Denmark. Under international law, both Canada and Denmark have the right to claim Hans Island as part of their countries because it falls within 12 miles (19.3 kilometers) of the Canadian shore to the south and within 12 miles of the Danish shore to the north.

Both countries agreed on the name of the channel after the British naval officer and arctic explorer George Strong Nares, but they cannot agree on who should get Hans Island, so both countries claim it!

In 1973, Canada and Denmark (on behalf of Greenland) signed a border treaty over Nares Strait, but neither country wanted to give up Hans Island, so they left a gap in the treaty on the Island's place on the border. Then, in 1984, a Canadian military ship went to the island and planted the Canadian flag and placed a bottle of Canadian whisky. Hearing of this, Denmark's Minister of Greenland Affairs went to the island to plant the Danish flag and left a bottle of schnapps and a letter written in Danish that said, "Welcome to the Danish Island". With both countries' flags and national alcoholic drinks, it was settled: Hans Island belonged to both of them.

This disagreement, sometimes called the "Whisky Wars", has not had any real impact for either country because no one lives on the Island. If they were to share the Island and have joint ownership, it would be possible. In fact, it would not be the first time an island would belong to two countries that do not share a land border. The Caribbean island of Saint Martin is divided between the Netherlands and France. Named Sint Maarten on the Dutch side and Saint-Martin on the French side, the island is divided in two in every aspect. The population on either side are citizens of either country, and each side has its own capital city: Philipsburg on the Dutch side, and Marigot on the French side. Hans Island's divide would be much easier because there are no cities and citizens to worry about.

In 2018, Canada and Denmark agreed to use geological exploration to find out which country is the rightful owner of Hans Island, and in 2019, both countries gave permission to a Canadian geologist to go on the exploration to solve the dispute once and for all. There has also been pressure from the other countries that share the borders of the Arctic Ocean and the Pacific Ocean to force Canada and Denmark to make a border because if they keep leaving Hans Island, someone else might come claim it, and they would all have to go to war. The decision on Hans Island is important now more than ever because if any other country left its flag on the island or set up a military base, both Canada and Denmark will be easy targets if a war broke out!

Operation: Acoustic Kitty

The 1960s were a period of recovery for the whole world, but more especially for the countries that had suffered major losses during World War II. In this time, countries that did not exist before the World War suddenly existed, others that used to be one big country were split into smaller countries, and friends and enemies had become less obvious. As the only country that was not physically destroyed by the War because none of the fights were ever within its borders, the United States of America came out ahead of most nations.

The 1960s also fell within the Cold War where the United States and the Soviet Union were always trying to outsmart each other. The United States' Central Intelligence Agency (CIA) was working on many experiments at the time to gain as much knowledge on foreign secret services as possible to better prepare for possible attacks and to be able to attack these foreign countries too. These experiments went from building bombs and training agents to disarm bombs to experimenting with human behaviors and how to gain control of people's minds.

The CIA and other countries' intelligence agencies had tried to use animals as spies before because they assumed their enemies and targets would not be suspicious of animals. They also had some studies from during World War II that some countries like Russia and Britain had used animals in their fighting, and some of the designs were good ideas, just used poorly. They had somewhere to start in creating smart wartime animals.

"Operation: Acoustic Kitty" was created to design and build a cat that could spy on foreign officials without them knowing to give the United States their secrets and plans. The cat was supposed to be a super cat with elements of a real cat and some technology like a cyborg cat. It had to be able to record and transmit conversations, take videos and pictures, and be able to pick up reception and location of its target, all while looking like a real, normal cat.

The CIA scientists spent five years planning and experimenting with different ways to use real cats to put all the technology needed, and it was a long and cruel process. Scientists would slit the cat open at different places, place batteries and all the transmitting devices, then sew up the wounds. They also had to wait for the cat to heal to avoid them having suspicious scars. Then they would train the cat to do certain things when they were given instructions.

Finally, after many tries that failed because cats just do what they want, they thought they had solved all the issues and sent out the first live test. The first Cyber Kitty was sent out to spy on two men sitting on a bench in a park, and the cat wandered out into a street near the park where it was hit by a taxi and destroyed. This project that had cost over $20 million failed all because no matter how smart, a cat always does what a cat wants.

Golf on the Moon

The United States' Apollo space program was a project that lasted for three years and sent twelve American astronauts to the Moon before humans had been to the Moon. The program was seven manned missions in total, and only one did not make it to the Moon. The first Apollo mission was Apollo 11 in 1969, and the last mission was Apollo 17 in 1972. While these missions were highly dangerous and very scary because we did not know what to expect, there were some silly and fun moments as well. The most famous was when the commander of the Apollo 14 mission swung two golf balls in space, becoming the first person to play golf on the Moon.

Apollo 11 was the first time that humans set foot on the Moon, and this became one of human history's greatest achievements. With the confidence and knowledge brought back by astronauts Neil Armstrong, Michael Collins, and Edwin Aldrin Jr., the National Aeronautics and Space Administration (NASA) of the government of the United States of America was preparing to launch more missions to the Moon and explore even more of space. People all over the world were very excited that human beings were smart and innovative enough to find a way to leave Earth and go to the Moon. Everyone was also very proud because we found out a lot of new information about the Moon and space. We also got to see the earth from the Moon, and this taught us a lot of important things about the Earth.

This led to Apollo 13, the second human mission meant to land on the Moon which resulted in an explosion that almost became the biggest space tragedy in our history. This is the mission from which the now famous echo of commander of the mission, James Lovell's voice which can be heard saying: "Houston, we've had a problem". The mission never made it to the Moon, but crew members Fred Haise, Jack Swigert, and James Lovell returned to Earth safely after the explosion, but there was clearly a lot of work to be done to prevent a similar incident and to make sure there was a safer and better way to go to space. The whole world wanted to see more space missions and Moon landings, and they were counting on NASA to do it.

NASA spent some time working on the new design for the spacecraft to make sure it was safer than the last one, and on January 31, 1971, they were ready for lift-off on another human mission to the Moon. This mission was named Apollo 14, and the commander astronaut was Alan Sheppard, who had been the first American in space in 1961. The other two crew members were Stuart Roosa and Edgar Mitchell.

Allan Sheppard liked playing golf, and when he had done the scientific work he was supposed to do, he took out a makeshift golf club he had put in his sock and two golf balls. Because of the heavy spacesuit, he could only swing with one hand and the first ball did not go very far. He hit the second ball, and it went a little further but still not very far. All of this was on live television with millions of people watching from Earth.

The Galloping Crocs of the Sahara Desert

The Sahara Desert is the third biggest desert in the world after the Arctic and Antarctic deserts. This makes the Sahara the biggest hot desert in the world. The Sahara is on the continent of Africa and is very hot compared to other parts of the world, even other deserts since they can get very cold in the night and winter. However, it was not always like this, and there was even a time when the climate of the areas in and around the Sahara was much wetter and cooler. Different kinds of crocodiles could live there, and they could all swim *and* gallop like horses!

The northern parts of the Sahara desert is where we find countries like Morocco, Niger, and Egypt, and you could find the galloping crocodiles in these places around the time of dinosaurs. Archaeologists found five skeletons of these crocodiles in the parts of the desert now in Morocco and Niger, and these skeletons tell the interesting and exciting story of the galloping crocodiles that not only lived with dinosaurs but also ate them.

One of the new species found is named *Kaprosuchus saharicus* and had three tusks that looked like daggers, a protected nose, and was 21.32 feet (6.5 meters) long. The other species was the same length but had a flat head and is named *Laganosuchus thaumastos*. This species is said to have moved in the water with its jaw open, ready to bite down on fish that would swim into its mouth without realizing it was a trap. The third species is named *Araripesuchus rattoides*, and it was 3.28 inches (1 meter) long and is believed to have had downward-pointing teeth that allowed it to dig for food.

The crocodiles ate different things and behaved differently because they lived in different sections of the desert. They also had some differences in their bodies. One of the species had a wide nose that could smell prey in the water, and the other had a soft nose like a dog's, probably to breathe better when moving fast whether underwater or on the ground. They also had many things in common as well. They were all clearly reptiles but had longer legs that allowed them to run on land, and they would have also been very fast. They had very strong and flexible tails that made them good at paddling, so they were also really good swimmers, and this was passed down to the crocodiles we have today, the galloping not so much.

Ancient Rome's Many Uses of Urine

Historical sources from both the Roman and Greek Empires have recorded instances of people using urine—human and animal—to whiten their teeth. One source even says that the Romans used to buy urine from the Portuguese to use as teeth whitener!

There are two groups of historians who say slightly different things about this matter, and both sides show us why they are probably the correct side.

On the one hand, historians say that because this information comes to us through poems and tales, it is possible and very likely that it is not true at all. We often say things that are not entirely true to make fun of people, and some people think that the poets who started writing about the Romans using urine to clean their teeth were doing just that. The earliest poet, Gaius Valerius Catullus, to write about this was speaking about a specific person who used urine to clean his teeth, and he was part of the Celtic group who lived in the central and eastern parts of the Iberian Peninsula and were under the rule of Roman Empire called the Celtiberians. The problem with this is that Catullus had never recorded visiting Celtiberian, so if he believed Celtiberians really used urine as mouthwash, he would have heard it from someone else and not seen it for himself. Additionally, Catullus was Italian Roman, and Italian Romans did not like Celtiberians and thought they were gross.

The other group of historians say that there may be some truth to it but also that we are not hearing the full story. These are the younger historians who are mostly reading and criticizing the works of the older and earlier historians. For example, the Greek historian Diodoros Sikeliotes also wrote about Celtiberians using urine but said that they both bathed in it and cleaned their teeth with it. Sikeliotes found this practise surprising because the Celtiberians were very clean. This version of events is also supported by Greek geographer Strabon of Amaseia.

So what has been proven?

All Catullus, Sikeliotes, and Strabon really tell us is that Celtiberians may have used urine to clean their teeth and bodies, but they cannot confirm if this is something that was done by all the Celtiberians. It is also hard to say if they did it all the time or if it was only done on certain occasions. We also do not know what the actual process was. Was the urine mixed with other things such as mint and other herbs or plants? What properties of the urine were important, and how did they know this?

If anything, their accounts tell us more about the Italian Romans and Greeks and how they looked down on the Celtiberians just because they did things differently from them. They could believe that people could put urine in their mouths because they did not think of the Celtiberians as people like them. Italian Romans themselves did use urine as bleach to clean their clothes, but they were not ridiculed for this.

Potatoes Can Grow in Space

Food is so important that we forget to even think about it. Eating is very much like breathing: Everyone does it, and we all have to eat to stay healthy and alive. There are many different kinds of diets and eating styles like vegetarian and pescatarian. Do you know what pescatarian means? Most of the food we eat comes from plants; there are people who do not eat meat and animal products like chicken nuggets, but everyone eats plants. You can also live a very long and healthy life eating only vegetables, and no other food group can say the same. Can you imagine eating only bread? Oh wait, bread is made from wheat—a plant!

Plants need gravity to know where downwards is so they can send their roots there to get nutrients in the soil and water. They also use gravity to send their shoots upwards so they can get enough light for photosynthesis to happen. There is no gravity in space, so the first thing scientists have to figure out is how to help plants grow without gravity. Controlled environment technologies create the same conditions that a plant would normally grow in to make the plant think it has everything it needs to grow, and plants themselves adapt and use other things such as light to grow if they cannot sense gravity in their environment.

Ag-Tec International, Ltd., an American agricultural technology development company based in Wisconsin, worked with the Wisconsin Center for Space Automation and Robotics at the University of Wisconsin-Madison, which is funded by NASA. Together they developed the technology that would allow astronauts to grow food in outerspace. They used an agricultural technique developed in China to create an environment that will be good for the plant to grow. Once the environment had been changed to encourage growth, it was time to get planting. The scientists chose potatoes because they are a sustainable and filling staple to many diets, and they also taste good!

The seeds were put inside tubes that use technology and computers to grow plants. The lighting inside these tubes is almost the same as natural sunlight, and they could control the temperature and water to make it the best environment to grow the potatoes. These tubes were also made to be used indoors, so you could grow potatoes the whole year and anywhere no matter what the weather outside is like. If you can grow potatoes in space, you can grow potatoes in the desert, in Antarctica, and just about anywhere.

This technology solves the basic problems farmers face such as unpredictable weather changes which can cause droughts and floods, bacteria and pests that can kill the plants, and low yield because plants are taking too long to grow. With this technology, you no longer have to wait for it to be summer for the plants to grow. It took anywhere between 40 and 50 days for the potatoes to be fully grown and ready to eat. It also solves the problem of small harvest because there is not enough space and machinery to grow a lot of plants at the same time, and the soil needs time to rest. The chambers used to grow potatoes in space could produce millions of minitubers a year. Most importantly, they were able to grow healthy and tasty potatoes. Since then, growing food for the astronauts to eat has become more popular, and they can now grow all kinds of lettuces, kale, and beautiful flowers.

Australia's Great Emu War

In 1932, about twenty thousand emus ran around causing chaos and disorder in the wheat farms of the Western territory of Campion, Australia. To try and control the emus, the Australian government sent soldiers to fight the emus, and this became known as the Great Emu War.

The emu is the second largest bird after the ostrich, and like its cousin ostrich, it also does not fly very high. Emus are indigenous to Australia, meaning they can only be naturally found in Australia.

The emus were ripping apart gardens, yards, fences, and anything in their way. This was a problem because many farmers live here, and the emus were ruining everything they needed to farm wheat. The animals that had been kept behind the farmers' fences escaped and also caused chaos of their own. The farms were not only being attacked by the emus but by their own animals as well. Broken fences also allowed in wild animals like the kangaroos, and this was not good for the farmers at all.

Many of the farmers who had wheat farms in these areas had been in World War I and didn't really have work, so the Australian government gave them land to farm wheat. As trained soldiers with rifles, the farmers set out to hunt and kill all the emus themselves, but they couldn't do that because they didn't have the kinds of ammunition they needed for their guns.

The confused and slightly frightened farmers didn't know

what to do because they needed the food that the emus were destroying in order to make money and for their families to eat. So they called on the government for help, and the government sent out the national military. These new soldiers were supposed to hunt and kill all the emus with machine guns. This seemed like a silly thing to do, sending out an army to kill birds!

While the soldiers prepared for their hunt of the emus, the farmers tried to herd the emus into a group to keep the emus all in one place so that the soldiers had a better chance at hunting them. After a few shots, the guns that the soldiers had brought locked up, and all of the emus broke free. The soldiers kept trying to come up with ways to kill the emus including trying to drive them over in trucks, but the emus were just too fast, and they scattered themselves in all directions to make it even harder to get them. The newspapers found the soldiers silly and made fun of them for being outsmarted by birds. One newspaper wrote the following:

> "The emus have proved that they are not so stupid as they are usually considered to be. Each mob has its leader, always an enormous black-plumed bird standing fully six-feet high, who keeps watch while his fellows busy themselves with the wheat. At the first suspicious sign, he gives the signal, and dozens of heads stretch up out of the crop. A few birds will take fright, starting a headlong stampede for the scrub, the leader always remaining until his followers have reached safety."

After suffering an embarrassing and public loss to emus, the government gave the farmers the ammunition they needed to shoot the emus, and in 1934, 57,034 emus were killed over six months. After this, the government called off the Great Emu War and just accepted that the emus would do whatever they wanted.

Today, there are over 700,000 emus in Australia, and the emu is on Australia's coat of arms alongside the kangaroo.

The Emperor Scared of Rabbits

Napoleon Bonaparte was one of the greatest emperors France has had. He was also a really strong and brave soldier who led many big battles during the Revolutionary Wars after the French Revolution. Even a man as great and fearless as Napoleon must have some fears, right? Many brave people are scared of big scary things like bears and tigers. Not Napoleon. His fear was…bunnies!

How did the bravest man in history become known as scared of soft, fluffy, cute bunnies?

Well, Napoleon and his army had just won a war, and he felt like celebrating with his men, and apparently hunting rabbits was a good way to celebrate winning a war in the 1800s in France. Because Napoleon was such a busy man, he did not go out to fetch the bunnies himself but sent his chief to find the rabbits.

This was a big mistake that would change how everyone saw Napoleon as a general in the future, and he went about his day, not knowing that the next day would be the most stressful day, maybe even more stressful than any war he had fought in. Napoleon had told his chief to only get a dozen bunnies, but the chief went out and came back with what seemed like anywhere between 700 to 3,000 bunnies. There were so many bunnies!

As a leader who had never backed out of a challenge, Napoleon went ahead with the hunting despite there being more bunnies than he wanted. On the morning of the hunt, all the bunnies were put in a cage, waiting for Napoleon and his men to start shooting at them. Then when they were ready, Napoleon and his men gave the instruction to let the bunnies out of the cage so they could start running away, then Napoleon would be able to hunt them. But something unexpected happened. Instead of running away, all 3,000 bunnies started running directly towards Napoleon.

Scared out of his mind, Napoleon and his men tried everything to get the rabbits to run the other way but the bunnies just kept charging at him. The bunnies attacked Napoleon and his men and they tried to 'shoo' them away but simply could not control the bunnies. Feeling defeated, Napoleon ran away and went into his carriage to escape the bunnies, and that just made the bunnies even more upset. As Napoleon was climbing into the back of his carriage, the bunnies began biting and scratching at his legs. Outnumbered, Napoleon began trying to close the door of the carriage, but historians say some of the bunnies climbed into the carriage with him before he could shut them out.

Historians who tell the story have even said that rabbits were being flung out of the windows of the carriage. These bunnies were everywhere, and no one could stop them until finally the coachmen dashed out of the area and carried Napoleon away in his cart.

All the bunnies wanted was probably some carrots to nibble on and maybe to not get killed, but they ended up standing up for themselves and actually attacking the most feared man in French history. It serves Napoleon and his men right for wanting to kill the fluffy, adorable bunnies.

Death by Cherries

Have you heard of the twelfth president of the United States of America President Zachary Taylor before? He is the only president in the history of the United States, and probably of the whole wide world, to die from eating cherries!

President Zachary Taylor died on July 9, 1850 after only being president for less than two years. At the time, no one knew what had killed him, but it was later said that he had died from a stomach disease caused by the bowl of cherries and iced milk he had been eating and drinking at the Fourth of July celebrations in Washington, D.C. where the Washington Monument was going to be built to celebrate America's freedom.

So how did President Taylor die by eating a bowl of cherries and drinking milk? Well, let's take a look at his last few days of life. The first of his five final days began on the Fourth of July where President Taylor was out celebrating all day. July is right in the middle of summer in the Americas, and it was very hot on this day. Historians say that President Taylor was drinking lots of milk with ice in it to keep cool throughout the day. And he was also snacking on berries at the Fourth of July celebration he went to. It is also very possible that he was drinking some water to quench his thirst from the heat.

At the end of the day, President Taylor decided to take a nice, long and relaxing walk along a river by himself to clear his head from the day's stress. After a nice walk, he returned to the White House and suddenly fell ill. He was quickly taken to bed, and the White House staff helped him get comfortable until a doctor could come see him. Over the next four days, President Taylor suffered from really bad cramping in his stomach, nausea, diarrhea, and all of this left him with dehydration. He died on the evening of July 9th.

This is where the story gets even more interesting.

The straightforward and simple explanation is that he died from the chemical reaction that happened in his stomach when the cherries mixed with the milk. Cherries have a lot of acid in them naturally, and when milk gets too hot, it turns bad and sour and makes acid. Our stomachs also have lining with some more acid. The acid in our stomachs is good because it kills the bad bacteria that's in the food we eat and helps the good bacteria in our gut to grow. Too much acid in the stomach is very bad and leads to a disease called gastroenteritis, which some people thought was what killed President Taylor.

The final report from President Taylor's doctor said that the President died from *cholera morbus*, and this also makes sense!

America in the 1800s had a big problem with water because the sewage system was very poorly built and unhygienic. There was an outbreak of cholera almost every summer because it was so hot. Cholera is an infectious disease caused by bacteria in the small intestine you can get from poor water supplies. This disease causes nausea and diarrhea, symptoms President Taylor had. He could have gotten the bacteria from the water he drank and the cubes of ice in his milk. Cholera is no longer as deadly as it used to be because doctors realized that because you lose so much fluid when you have nausea and diarrhea, the quickest way to get better is to drink more fluids.

See? No need to say "no thank you" to tasty cherry pie or a nice cold glass of milk with your cookies in the summer because, thankfully, the water supplies in most countries have been made much better now, and we have clean, safe water to drink. And if you visit very hot countries where you are at risk of drinking water that might make you sick, there are pills you can put into your water to kill the bacteria that causes cholera. You can enjoy cherries, milk, and water anywhere in the world because of the amazing and smart work scientists and doctors have done since the time of President Zachary Taylor.

Naps Save Lives

It is very important to get a good night's sleep every night. In fact, children need between nine and twelve hours of sleep every night to be refreshed and have enough energy to get through the day. If you do not get enough sleep for too many nights, you start to wake up groggy and tired everyday, and this is no fun. You can't play with your friends, and you will also not be able to do simple things like pay attention and listen when people speak to you. This happens to adults too, but when they don't get enough sleep or sleep on the job, disasters can happen.

On January 28, 1986, in Cape Canaveral, Florida, a spacecraft called the *Challenger* that was headed on a very important space mission fell apart just 73 seconds after leaving the ground to take off to go to space. All seven crew members inside the *Challenger* died as the pieces of the spacecraft fell into the Atlantic Ocean. The mechanics and personnel teams that were working on the spaceship were working day and night to make sure the mission happened. Sometimes, they would be at work from the start of the day to the end of the day without taking breaks to eat or even talk to their friends. They were doing very important work and simply did not have the time to waste on other things, and they also could not fix mistakes in time because they were working so fast.

Ironically, the fact that workers were given too much work to do in a short time because NASA wanted to launch many missions in a short time was one of the many reasons for this accident. Greed and sleep deprivation were some of the reasons for the tragedy.

Another big accident that could have been avoided with a good night's sleep was the Exxon Valdez Spill, the worst environmental disaster in history.

On March 24, 1989, an oil tanker going to Long Beach California crashed into Bligh Reef near the coast of Prince William Sound in Alaska. The ship spilled 11 million gallons (42 million liters) of oil into the ocean. This trip was supposed to be made by Captain Joseph Hazelwood, but he had had a few drinks the night before and decided to let his third officer Gregory Cousins man the ship. Cousins had only had six hours of sleep in the last two days, and he was so tired that he hit a reef that they knew was there because they had done this trip hundreds of times. The ship called for help, but it could not come fast enough, and luckily no one died. Sadly, irreparable damage had been done to the animals and plants in that section of the ocean.

There's one more story to tell you just how important it is to get a good night's sleep. On June 1, 1999, at the Little Rock National Airport, an American Airline airplane Flight 1420 transporting 145 people from Dallas/Fort Worth International Airport to Little Rock National Airport overran the runway when it was landing and crashed into a building that was holding passengers waiting for their flights. This accident killed the captain of the flight and 10 passengers and injured about one hundred people. After the crash, the National Transportation Safety Board wanted to find out what went wrong, and they reported that the pilot and his co-pilot had been fatigued, and that was one of the things that caused the crash. After being awake for more than 13 hours, pilots make more mistakes.

So get all comfortable and snug in your bed and get some sleep as much as you can because you want to be wide awake so that you don't miss anything!

The Leaning Tower of Pisa—Never Straight

The Tower of Pisa is one of the most popular attraction sites in Europe and brings in many tourists to the city of Pisa in Italy. The city's name 'Pisa' is a Greek word meaning "marshy land." That means that the ground is soft, and heavy objects often sink into this mushy soil, but the leaning Tower of Pisa is not the only building that is either leaning or sinking. There are two smaller leaning bell towers at the churches of St. Michele dei Scalzi and the church of St. Nicola. The Cathedral of Pisa and the Baptistery of Pisa, which are both older than the Tower of Pisa, are also sinking. These magnificent buildings are all located in the *Piazza dei Miracoli*—Square of Miracles, in English—which was declared a World Heritage Site by the United Nations Educational, Scientific and Cultural Organization (UNESCO) in 1987. It is one of the remaining creations of medieval Europe built in the Roman architectural style.

The designer of the Tower of Pisa wanted it to be fully vertical, but it was built on an unstable foundation. That is why the Tower began to lean as they started adding floors. Construction of the leaning Tower of Pisa began in August of 1173, and it took over 199 years to finish. The Tower of Pisa was built in three phases, and the first phase of construction was led by sculptors Bonanno Pisano and Gherardo din Gherardo. The designer and architect of the Tower is unknown, and some even think there were more than one. Construction was stopped suddenly when the ground began to sink after the third floor of the Tower was built in 1178. This break ended up lasting one hundred years because during this time, the Republic of Pisa was battling with the neighboring republics of Genoa, Lucca, and the city of Florence. However, these battles seemed to actually help Pisa finish its Tower. This break was necessary for the soil to harden, making sure that the Tower stayed upright even though it had a visible tilt. Many historians have written that if construction had not been interrupted, the Tower would have never been completed.

The second phase of construction began in December of 1275, led by Giovanni di Simone. To try and make up for the tilt, the engineers working on the upper floors of the Tower built them with one side taller than the other. This phase was also interrupted in 1285 when the Republic of Pisa was defeated by the Republic of Genoa in the Battle of Meloria

Tommaso Pisano began the third and final phase of the construction of the Tower of Pisa, and this phase ended in 1399 with the complete tower.

Throughout the building process and even the years after construction was complete, the Tower continued to tilt and was at 5.5 degrees tilt in 1990. Fearing the collapse of the Tower, a team of engineers came up with a solution to keep the tower from falling over and make the foundation stable. This was in two stages, first through a process called soil extraction, where the engineers dug tunnels on the side of the tower that is not leaning to remove soil under the foundation. This would make the ground underneath the not leaning side start to sink and even out the Tower. The second process began when engineers realized that the Tower tilted more in winter because the water table on the north side was higher than on the south when it rained, causing the side to lift and increasing the tilt. To try and fix this, the engineers dug drains under the foundation so that water could flow out. The leaning Tower of Pisa was closed to the public during this time, and it was reopened in 2001, and engineers are confident it has another 200 years before it will tilt anymore.

Mansa Musa—The Richest Person in History

Did you know the wealthiest man in the history of the world was from the continent of Africa and had so much wealth that he messed up the economy of an entire country with his generosity? No, it is not T'Challa but Emperor of the West African Empire of Mali, Mansa Musa.

Mansa Musa was born to an extremely wealthy family in 1280 and inherited the kingdom in 1312 when his older brother, who was to succeed their father, went on an expedition across the Atlantic Ocean, never returning to Mali. Historians agree that there is no modern measure of Mansa Musa's riches, and it is very difficult to even imagine just how rich he was.

Mansa Musa was given the title of 'Mansa,' which means king, when he was crowned as emperor of Mali. Mali was one of the empires with enormous gold reserves as part of the West Africa gold coast alongside Ghana. They also traded salt, ostrich feathers, and slaves across the Sahara Desert to North Africa. Mansa Musa helped strengthen Mali's trades with other empires and even kept the trade route across the Sahara open.

After many years of planning, Mansa Musa—and 60,000 people that escorted him—began his famous pilgrimage to the holy city of Mecca in 1324. This journey is still practiced today and is known as the *hajj*. For Mansa Musa, this hajj was even more important because it was his way of building friendships with the other rulers that practiced Islam. Along the way, he stopped in Cairo, Egypt and gave away some of the gold he had brought with him. He gave so much gold away that his generosity devalued gold in Cairo. This means that there was so much gold that anyone could have it, making its worth and value decrease since nobody really wanted any more. It took the Egyptians at least 12 years to recover from the damage this caused on their gold market and economy. After he returned from his pilgrimage, Mansa Musa began to revitalize the cities in Mali, starting with Timbuktu.

Mansa Musa's home kingdom of Mali was not only famous for being one of the greatest and richest empires in history but also home to some of the oldest libraries in the world found in the city of Timbuktu. In fact, some of them are still there to this day. The Empire of Mali also has one of the earliest universities in the world, Sankoré (University of Timbuktu), where Malian scholars studied long before universities were common in Europe. The university thrived under Mansa Musa, and he built its library collections and hired scholars who made it a leading university and learning center. Mansa Musa died in 1337 after being emperor for 25 years, and he was succeeded by his son, Maghan I.

Lord Byron's Pet Bear

British poet and politician George Gordon Byron, 6th Baron Byron—also known as Lord Byron for short—is known for many things: his moving romanticism in poetry, imaginative and genius plays, and his ability to make strong political arguments. Oh! And his pet bear.

Lord Byron became a student at Cambridge's highly respected Trinity College in 1805 and immediately had a problem with the college's old and backwards rules. He was especially upset about their rules against dogs. Trinity College did not allow students and staff to have pet dogs on campus, and this annoyed Lord Byron enough to bring a tame bear to the college.

When college authorities tried to tell Lord Byron that he could not keep a pet bear, he directed them to the college's rule book to argue that since bears were not specifically named as banned animals, the college could not legally ban his pet bear. He won the fight and was allowed to keep his pet bear at the school. He would take his pet on walks on the college grounds, using a leash as if he were walking a dog. In an 1807 letter to his friend, Lord Byron wrote: "I have got a new friend, the finest in the world, a tame bear. When I brought him here, they asked me what to do with him, and my reply was, 'He should sit for a fellowship.'" After graduating from Trinity College, Lord Byron took his pet bear to his home of Newstead Abbey, where he had a tame wolf roaming the grounds of his ancestral home.

This behavior was not out of character for Lord Byron because he loved to argue, and he loved animals so much that he had many, many pets throughout his life. According to Lord Byron, his favorite pet he ever had was a Newfoundland called Boatswain. He loved this dog so much that when Boatswain caught rabies, Lord Byron nursed him without worrying about his own safety. When Boatswain died, a monument was built in his honor, and Lord Byron wrote one of his most famous poems "Epitaph to a Dog" for Boatswain. He also expressed his wish to be buried next to his dog when he died. In addition to popular domestic animals such as dogs and cats, he is also said to have kept a crocodile, monkeys, a honey badger, a fox, peacocks, and various birds of prey.

Animals of WWII—Juliana the Great Dane

In 1941, Britain was under constant attack and air raids by Germany during World War II. These bombings were targeted at cities, towns, and industrial areas and destroyed two million homes, killing over 40,000 people and injuring thousands. On one occasion, an incendiary bomb fell through the roof and into a house that a Great Dane named Juliana lived in with her owner. With no military training, Juliana went over to the bomb and peed on it, extinguishing the bomb before it could detonate.

Juliana was awarded the Blue Cross medal for this brave act that not only saved her owner's life but possibly the lives of the people around their house who would have been affected by the blast of the incendiary bomb. The Blue Cross medal is an award to honor animals and people who have changed or saved lives. The first Blue Cross medals awarded to animals were awarded to the horses that served in World War I in 1918, and Juliana was one of the first dogs to be honored with this award during the Second World War.

Three years later, Juliana committed another act of bravery when she alerted her owner of a fire that had started in the owner's shoe shop. Juliana's quick acting got all the people out before the fire engulfed the shop, and not a single life was lost. She was honored with a second Blue Cross medal. Sadly, Juliana the Great Dane died from poison in her owner's mailbox in 1946, a year after World War II ended.

Juliana's story was forgotten until a property clearing in Bristol, England in 2013. An auctioneer found the 1941 Blue Cross medal and a painting of Juliana with a plaque describing how she extinguished an incendiary bomb during the war. Both items were estimated to sell for about £60 but sold for £1,100 instead.

The Great Dane is not Danish despite its name, and is, in fact, German. The Great Dane gained popularity as a hunting dog and many of the early writings about the dog breed said it was Danish or implied a link to Denmark. This was not received well by Nazi Germany, and during World War II, the German dog society under Nazi control, *Reichsverband für das Deutsche Hundewesen*, tried to have the Great Dane renamed to *Duetche Dogge* which means German Dog. Even though the dog was called this in the German federation, it was still known as the Great Dane to pretty much the rest of the world, and this attempted renaming failed.

Animals of WWII—Exploding Rats

There are many stories of animals being involved in wars throughout history. Many of the early battles across the world were often fought on horseback. Other animals such as mules were useful in providing support and transport to legions crossing the deserts of North Africa and the Middle East. Dogs are probably the most documented and credited animals for their work in the police field because most police stations have a canine (K-9) unit. Dogs have even been used for various tasks in both World Wars. As watchdogs, they would use their senses of smell and hearing to warn the soldiers of approaching danger. As combat dogs, they would be trained to attack the enemy. As rescue dogs, they would carry medical supplies to wounded soldiers under attack. More specialized dogs were used to send messages between different camps, and some were trained as sniffer dogs to find landmines and people buried under debris after bombings.

These animals were relying on their own skills and abilities to successfully save lives and help others save lives during conflict. They had to be alive for them to do their jobs. As it seemed like Germany was winning the war and getting very close to destroying Britain, the British World War II secret forces had to think of a plan to survive quickly. They thought using an animal would give them the advantage and began thinking of the perfect animal to carry out this important work. Their decision? The rat bomb. To create these special tools, a real rat would be skinned, and then the skin would be sewn back to form the shape of a living rat. The rat skin would be filled with plastic explosives that would then fill out its shape and look like a rat to the unsuspecting eye.

The plan was to deposit the rats in Germany's coal supplies so that they would make their way into homes, military bases, steam engines, and pretty much anywhere people were using coal, and explode, destroying these structures. This would destroy industries such as food suppliers and would cause panic across Germany. This panic and destruction would allow Britain to conquer Germany because their military bases would be weakened.

This did not work out as Britain had hoped, and somehow the Germans discovered the first batch of these rat bombs before some had even been unknowingly distributed. Britain's mission had failed, and the rat bombs joined the list of failed animal-like bombs like the cat bomb and bat bombs.

Albert Einstein and Israeli Politics

Albert Einstein is known in most parts of the world as possibly one of the smartest people of all time. His discovery of the law of the photoelectric effect won him the 1921 Nobel Prize in Physics and opened up a whole new world for quantum physics. Einstein was clearly an intelligent man, so why did he say no when he was asked to be the president of the state of Israel in 1952? Einstein's exact words declining the offer were the following:

> "I am deeply moved by the offer from our State of Israel [to serve as President], and at once saddened and ashamed that I cannot accept it. All my life I have dealt with objective matters, hence I lack both the natural aptitude and the experience to deal properly with people and to exercise official functions."

The offer to become the president of the State of Israel was made by the Prime Minister after the first president of Israel, Chaim Weizmann, died on November 9, 1952. The presidency in Israel is a symbolic position, a little like the Queen in England; They can and do make some decisions, but the Prime Minister is the person truly running the country. If Einstein had accepted the offer, he was expected to leave the United States of America where he was working as a professor at Princeton University to live permanently in Israel. The offer made it clear that he would still have the freedom to continue working in science since the job was not as demanding as the Prime Minister's job.

Einstein was likely offered the presidency of Israel because he was born to a Jewish family in Germany in 1879. Moreover, he shared some similar beliefs as the government and people of Israel. The State of Israel was formed in 1948 three years after the end of the Second World War as the first Jewish state in over 2,000 years. Israel recognizes Jewish people from all over the world and remains open to anyone of Jewish descent to claim citizenship, and that is why Einstein would have been able to serve as the president of Israel even though he was not born there, just like their first president. This makes this appointment unique because many states typically require a presidential candidate to have been born in that state and to have very clear roots in the communities of that country and its territories.

The Stolen Brain of Albert Einstein

German-born Nobel Prize-winning physicist Albert Einstein was aware of his contributions not only to the world of physics but to the world in general. He knew that it was not silly to think that people would want to keep and study his brain after his death to try to understand and explain why his brain worked the way it did. He is, after all, considered the most influential physicist of the 20th century. Towards the end of his life, he gave very clear and specific instructions that his body was to be cremated and his ashes scattered in secret to avoid people worshiping the place he would be buried in. He insisted that his brain and body should not be studied, but these wishes were not respected.

Einstein died on April 18, 1955 in Princeton Hospital at the age of 76, and the pathologist on call, Thomas Harvey, stole his brain. A few days after his death, it was discovered that Dr. Harvey had taken his brain without Einstein's family's permission or any written consent from Einstein himself. As a last resort, Einstein's son Hans Albert gave Dr. Harvey permission to study the brain as long as it was strictly for science. With this forced blessing, Dr. Harvey took the brain with him to Philadelphia when he lost his job in Princeton. This was the first of many moves, and Einstein's brain moved around a lot and was often stored in unusual places. Throughout this time, Dr. Harvey was dissecting and studying the brain.

In Philadelphia, Dr. Harvey divided the pieces of the brain into two jars and stored them in his basement. While he was away working, his wife threatened to throw the brain out, and he went back to take it with him to his new job in Kansas, where he kept the brain in a cider box under a beer cooler. Things did not work out there either, and he moved to Weston Missouri where he practiced medicine again, studying the brain in his spare time. He lost his medical license in 1988 and moved back to Kansas.

Harvey sent pieces of Einstein's brain to scientists all over the world, and most of them agreed that the brain was not normal, but no one could point to a feature that could explain Einstein's genius. After all that trouble and work, the mystery still wasn't solved. So what exactly was found in the brain? Albert Einstein's brain weighed less than the average adult male's brain, had a thinner cerebral cortex than that of five brains used to compare, and had a greater density of neurons compared to the average male. But there was also one big problem with these studies: They had only Albert Einstein's brain to compare. Without the other brains of people with high mathematical and intellectual abilities, we aren't able to say that these differences in Einstein's brain are the main cause of geniusness.

If you're ever curious about what his brain looked like, there are places that it is scattered and put on display. The best place to go is the Mütter Museum of the College of Philadelphia.

Sir Isaac Newton and the Apple

Do you ever wonder why things in the world work the way they do? The last time someone wondered why apples always fall straight down to the ground and not upwards or sideways, an important scientific discovery was made. Sir Isaac Newton's law of universal gravitation was the basic principle that inspired his three laws of motion. Many great scientific discoveries of the time were discovered by observation and not always experimenting. Scientists made discoveries just by going about their daily lives, and many of the laws of physics were discovered this way. Whether Sir Isaac Newton was sitting under the tree from which the apple fell or whether the apple touched his head we do not know, but I imagine it must have been very funny if the apple did indeed land on his head.

It is important to remember that although Sir Isaac Newton made his important discovery by 'accident,' he was more than qualified to make that observation, and that is why people believed him when he told them about the principle and how he discovered it. Sir Isaac Newton began his education at Cambridge University in 1661 where he studied law. His studies were interrupted by the bubonic plague, and Cambridge University temporarily closed due to the highly contagious disease. During this time, Sir Isaac Newton went back to his childhood home and began to develop his own ideas on physics, math, astronomy, and optics. It was during this time away from university that he made the discovery that would make him one of the most respected scientists in history.

Sir Isaac Newton made many other important discoveries and inventions throughout his life. He invented the reflecting telescope and created a cool theory of color that we use to this day. He also came up with the first calculation for the speed of sound. His achievements as a mathematician also include inventing calculus, although he did not publish it immediately. In addition, he added on to the study of power series and many other functions of mathematics. Sir Isaac Newton died a highly respected physicist and mathematician in 1727 at the age of 84 and was buried at Westminster Abbey. The famous apple tree that gave the world the most important laws on motion is still growing in his father's orchard in Woolsthorpe Manor.

Man had Hiccups for 68 Years

There is a Guinness World Record for the longest attack of hiccups, and it is held by a man named Charles Osborne of Iowa, United States of America. Born in Anthon, Iowa in 1893, Charles led a normal life until an accident at work changed his life at the age of 28. Charles used to work at a butchery and fell while trying to hang a 350 pound hog for slaughtering. At the time, he reported not feeling like anything was wrong or broken, but some years later, a doctor told him that his fall had resulted in the bursting of a blood vessel and had caused damage to the part of the brain that prevents hiccup response. Charles started to hiccup almost immediately after the fall, and the hiccups went on for the next 68 years.

In the beginning, Charles hiccuped 40 times in one minute, and this went on for the first few decades. Eventually, he became so tired of hiccuping that he began to travel the world to look for a cure. As time went by, Charles stopped trying to find a solution because the costs were too great, and he made the decision to live as normal a life as possible with the hiccups. He learned how to breathe mindfully to quiet most of the noise from his hiccups and to manage and reduce them 20 hiccups per minute. When he was sleeping, the hiccups went away.

Charles lived a normal life, was married twice, and had eight children. He played cards with his friends and went on his morning walks almost every day. In one occasion, Charles tells the story of how, while playing cards, one of his friends made a loud noise behind him, hoping that the hiccups would stop if he got really scared. He was right about the *really scared* part, but sadly the hiccups did not go away. My grandfather once told me that the quickest way to get rid of hiccups is to ask the person with hiccups "When was the last time you saw a white horse?" It works every time, unless they have recorded 40 hiccups in the last minute!

In the last decade of his life, Charles could no longer eat whole foods in between the hiccups and had to blend all his food. It was the only way he could eat without sucking it up and choking on it. Then, in February of 1990, after 68 years of constant hiccuping and about 430 million hiccups later, the hiccups miraculously stopped. Charles was 96 years old at the time, and he lived for one more year. In total, he was free of hiccups for only 29 years of his long life.

The Mad Doctor—Dr. Semmelweis

Handwashing is the most important way to ensure we stop germs from sneaking into our bodies. We wash our hands before and after we eat, after playtime, and pretty much any time we have been outside or have held anything that might have germs on it. We wash our hands whenever we use the bathroom, sneeze, and especially when we feel sick. Almost two hundred years ago, washing your hands was not as popular as it is today, and even doctors would work with their patients without cleaning their hands and equipment. The story of handwashing begins with Hungarian doctor Ignaz Semmelweis in Vienna, where he was in charge of two maternity wards in a hospital in Vienna.

Dr. Semmelweis was born July 1, 1818 and became a doctor in a time where many mothers were dying after childbirth due to childbed fever. As an obstetrician, or a doctor that specializes in taking care of pregnant mothers and delivering babies, Dr. Semmelweis noticed a difference in mortality rates in two different maternity wards. The difference was the hygiene practices in the two wards. Fewer mothers died in the ward where midwives were helping deliver babies than in the ward where doctors and medical students were delivering babies. The only difference was that the doctors and medical students' ward was close to the autopsy room, and it was common for doctors to go from conducting autopsies to delivering babies without washing their hands. Midwives only helped deliver babies, so they didn't have the germs that came from doing surgery like the doctors and students did. In 1847, Dr. Semmelweis suggested that all doctors and medical students needed to wash their hands in a chlorine solution after conducting autopsies before handling patients and children. Despite it being clear that handwashing was saving lives, the doctors did not want to do it, and Dr. Semmelweis publicly exposed them for not washing their hands before treating patients.

The other doctors were upset with Dr. Semmelweis because they felt attacked and embarrassed but also did not want to admit that the patients' deaths were caused by poor hygiene and not a disease that was spread through the air like they were saying. In fact, Dr. Semmelweis was fired from the hospital he was working at in Vienna because they wouldn't listen to his ideas. He then moved to Budapest and started working at a new hospital where he continued to encourage the staff to wash their hands with chlorine before treating their patients. Even in this new job, he was mocked for his beliefs.

This upset Dr. Semmelweis, and he began to publicly write about the importance of handwashing in hospitals. When he was still mocked by the other doctors, his mental health suffered so severely that he could not talk about anything else but childbed fever and antiseptic practices. When he began showing symptoms of early onset dementia, he was tricked into visiting an asylum in 1865, thinking he was just going to tour the new facilities. When he realized that he was being admitted as a patient, he, in a fit of rage, tried to leave but was beaten by the guards at the asylum and thrown into a cell. Mental health was not treated with care and sensitivity back then, and he was humiliated and mistreated throughout his stay, and he died two weeks after being admitted. It is said that he sustained an injury from the beating, and it got infected. Almost 20 years after his death, Dr. Semmelweis' ideas about antiseptic practices were adopted in all the world's hospitals and continue to be the most important practices in public healthcare.

The benefits of handwashing are not only seen in healthcare but in our daily lives. By practicing good hygiene that promotes handwashing with soap and water, we have been able to help the fight against global outbreaks of diseases and viruses and have collectively saved many lives. In our schools, we are taught to always wash our hands and to take care of babies, the elderly, the sick, and anyone who might get very sick from germs because of Dr. Semmelweis' discovery. It's thanks to him that we can go about our lives healthy and germ-free!

Say "Cheese!" Now Hold for 8 Hours

Imagine having to sit still and hold a smile for eight hours for one picture on school picture day! Well, that is exactly what would have happened if you were going to school in the 1820s. The first image on a camera took eight hours to capture and a few days to develop, and the quality wasn't even that good. It was not until 1839 that an earlier version of the camera we use today was first introduced, developing images from a camera in minutes and producing clear, finely detailed images.

Today we take pictures from instant polaroid cameras and get them immediately, and we can also take very high quality pictures with phones and other gadgets like tablets and iPads. However, photography was not always so easy and quick. Before cameras were invented, people used a box with a hole that allowed light to come in through one side and hit a mirror placed inside. This was called camera obscura, which means "dark chamber." An image of any object placed in front of the light hole would be captured inside the box, but this image was only there for as long as there was light, and disappeared when the light disappeared. Camera obscura was an important invention that gave us an idea of how light actually works to reproduce images, and this was the birth of photography.

The word 'photography' comes from two Greek words: *fos* (light) and *grafo* (to write). Once they understood that photography was basically writing with light, scientists Joseph Niepce and Louis Daguerre began to work out how to take photographs that would not disappear with the light. Joseph Niepce took the world's oldest photograph in 1826 when he put his camera on the windowsill to record the view outside his house. It took eight hours for the image to form, and it was blurry, but it still exists to this day. Louis Daguerre was also experimenting with photography around the same time and made photography more accessible. Daguerre came up with a technique to capture photographs called daguerreotypes, and they took over 20 minutes to be captured. Needless to say this was much shorter than Niepce's eight hours to take a single photograph!

The main challenge was making sure the pictures did not fade, and many scientists tried over many years to fix this by using different chemicals, paper, metals, and other surfaces. Finally, in 1880, George Eastman invented camera film, starting with paper film and then celluloid film later. Eastman is famous for inventing the first small handheld box camera which he named the 'Kodak.' Yes, *that* Kodak. In 1888, the first Kodak was sold, and the cameras were small enough to carry around and contained a 100-exposure roll of film that used paper negatives. To develop and print the pictures, and reload the film, the whole camera had to be sent to the manufacturer. Although more advanced and much quicker, we still use many of the original ideas and techniques of photography today.

The next time you take a selfie, hold the pose for as long as you can to see if you would have been able to sit still with the same smile for picture day if you were born in the 1800s. Because even the slightest movement would have resulted in a blurry, poorer quality image, it may work best if you do not blink and breathe very gently the whole time!

Captain Jack Sparrow was a Girl

Ching Shih was born Shi Yang in 1775, Guangdong Province, China and lived in the Chinese city of Canton under the Qing Dynasty before becoming a pirate. In 1801, at 26 years old, she married a notorious pirate named Cheng I whose operations ran in the South China Sea. Cheng I was the fearsome commander of pirate ships known as the Red Flag Fleet and had been successful in uniting many Chinese pirate groups who had been fighting. Ching Shih participated in Cheng I's piracy and succeeded him when he died. She became Ching Shih (meaning "Cheng's widow") and began pillaging in Canton.

Ching Shih was a very persuasive and skilled businesswoman who used the secrets of her husband's clients to gain more power. As a condition to agreeing to marry Cheng I, she wanted equal power and control of the Red Flag Fleet and soon became the head of the organization. When Cheng I died in 1807, his successor Cheung Po Tsai was supposed to take over the Red Flag Feet, and this placed Ching Shih in a dangerous position. It was very rare to find female pirates, let alone female leaders of fleets of pirate ships. Realizing she could lose everything, Ching Shih took Cheung Po Tsai as her lover and eventually married him. This put her back in power and at the height of her leadership, and she commanded over 1,800 ships and about 80,000 men.

Ching Shih made the pirates under her rule live by a very strict code of laws. These laws stated that orders could only come from a superior, and if a pirate disobeyed these orders or gave orders of their own, they would be beheaded. There were also clear laws about female captives and how they were to be treated. Any pirate who mistreated female captives was to be put to death. Furthermore, if a pirate married a captive, he could only have one wife (the captive). The pirates respected Ching Shih and followed the code of law and obeyed her authority. This was part of why the Red Flag Fleet was undefeated, even though Qing dynasty officials, the East India Company, and the Portuguese Navy tried to destroy it.

Ching Shih retired in 1810 after a successful three years in power, and she accepted the Chinese government's offer of amnesty. It is said that there was in-fighting in the Red Flag Fleet, and the pirates were no longer working together. She lived long for a pirate and died at the age of 69 in 1844. Today her legacy is best seen in the character of the Pirate Lord of the Pacific Ocean, Mistress Ching, inspired by her life in *Pirates of the Caribbean: At World's End*.

You may have only heard of pirates from stories and movies such as *Pirates of the Caribbean*, but piracy is still practiced to this day. Many of the pirate ships today do not look like the ships we read about, but they are inspired by real pirates of the past such as Cheng I and Ching Shih. In the oceans of the world, there is a whole world of pirates who live by the idea of a pirates' code introduced by Ching Shih over a thousand years ago, but the exact code of law depends on the specific pirate ship, the fleet they belong to, and the ocean they are operating in. Pirates still roam the seas, and if you search hard enough, you might just find a fleet or two.

Final Words

This book offers parents the freedom to pick any story any time and read to their children because none of the stories are related. It can also be a fun activity that allows them to involve their children in picking a story, perhaps a raffle or numbers game to decide which story to read. Moreover, the book is great for flexibility; you can read one story, or two, in one sitting, and there is no obligation to stick to a long story because each story begins sharply as new and clearly unrelated to the last one, and ends with a resolution and satisfying sense of completion. Your child will get to fully experience each story and will not be left wondering what happened or anticipating a follow-up story.

The stories are in a language simple and clear enough for all ages but also have some fun challenges which will most likely align with your child's educational development journey. In each story, there is an opportunity to learn a new word or two. In addition, each story has a light-hearted ending to look forward to, and the opening paragraphs give the assurance that it is not all gloomy. These skillfully planted life lessons allow the young reader to arrive at the important lesson by and for themselves, and offers the parents the opportunity to reinforce these lessons in a language that you know your child(ren) responds best to.

Without imposing a certain approach to introducing literature to children, this book encourages parents to let their children read as many of the stories for themselves out loud, as often as possible, narrating in silly voices and with the full use of their imaginations. This book allows them to color into what is often typically taught as grim history—dead and dull and reserved for school. It challenges them to find creative ways to bring these stories to life in the home and to get involved in creating and interpreting them.

Great care has gone into delivering factual, historically and contextually accurate information that is both sensitive and respectful of the people, places, and cultures discussed in this book. This book is underpinned by the strong belief in integrity and dignity in storytelling because the people in our tales are often not here to correct us if we make errors in our retelling of their life stories. As such, these stories are told with honesty and objectivity as far as possible, and compassion and an empathetic reading of history has taken over where little or unconvincing facts were found. The stories are deliberately extremely easy to follow but not watered down or oversimplified to honor the people and places they represent. You will find that even as an adult you may have never heard of many of these stories, so it is indeed a whole family feast. Enjoy learning about, laughing at, and celebrating our pasts, presents and futures.

Printed in Great Britain
by Amazon